Rapid
and
Reliable Analysis

Reinhold Ebertin

ISBN-10: 0-86690-093-4
ISBN-13: 978-0-86690-093-5

Cover Design: Jack Cipolla
Translator: Patrick Harding

Published by:
American Federation of Astrologers, Inc.
6535 S. Rural Road
Tempe, AZ 85283

Printed in the United States of America

Contents

Introduction

A well-known advocate of classical astrology once spoke these prophetic words: "Since the Shah has Mars in the eighth house he will die by assassination." This statement is, in its way, just as wrong as that made by another astrologer: "When Mars is in the seventh house, there is discord in the marriage." Let us also quote the following from the book by Brandler-Pracht: "This transit [of Mars] makes one angry, moody, restless, and inconsistent, and causes sudden and unexpected losses, accidents, sudden changes in all relationships, and attacks of fever."

These statements are all false because they are based upon an incorrect assumption. They lead one to believe that a star in a particular position is the cause of a future event, but this is not the case, at least not in such a context. This kind of statement probably originated from the "personification" of the stellar bodies, which was common centuries ago when people thought of Mars as the god and creator of war, or of Saturn as the guardian of the threshold and the god of death. These personifications are, however, incompatible with our modern way of thinking.

Of course I can say that it hurts if by accident I hit my finger with a hammer while knocking a nail into the wall; this is clearly a case of cause and effect. But one can never say that Mars in a certain position in the sky is the cause of an accident to this person or that.

One may find many things in the constellations, relationships, or parallels, but never the causes of earthly happenings.

One sees the confusion of many astrologers in the way they interpret a horoscope. On the one hand they rely upon the mythical and symbolic thought of previous ages and on "artistic intuition" to draw up and interpret a horoscope. On the other they try to build into their astrological thinking elements of materialistic thought, or in other words, the connection between cause and effect.

Professor Rudolf Tomaschek, in his paper "Cosmic Force Fields and Astral Influences," given at the tenth work conference of cosmobiological research at Aalen, asked, "Are the positions and movements of the stars the cause of the observed effect?"

The speaker based his talk upon the fact that "the structure of our scientific thinking forces us to the conclusion that every event in our spheres has adequate cause, but to find this cause is not at all simple or straightforward."

When a tile falls from the roof the reason lies in the force of gravity, which in its turn is caused by the great mass of our earth. But why did the tile not fall earlier? Why only now? It may have been moved by a gust of wind or by a bird.

So there was a triggering mechanism, which might have been the hopping of a little bird onto the tile, bears no relationship to the harm that the falling tile can cause. To illustrate this the speaker used the example of an ignition key that when turned can move a heavy car, and also the pressing of a button, which can unleash an atomic war of total annihilation. Professor Tomaschek concluded that "most of the stellar influence may be felt through this trigger mechanism rather than through a direct effect."

Following is further consideration of our example of the bird on the roof:

Through the passage of time and the effects of the weather a tile has become loose, a tiny shock causes it to fall, and in doing so the tile might break in too little pieces, damage a flower bed, or fall on someone's head and kill him. It is always a matter of relationship between the differing results and the various possible causes.

In the same way we must consider the problem of the effect of the triggering mechanism of the stellar influences upon human life. The cosmic birth chart of a person is the prime factor, but in addition to this there are inherited tendencies and environmental influences. So great differences are apparent in character and development of people born to the same mother because of the influence of factors other than cosmic ones. We can thus assume that the cosmic factors cannot be considered in isolation but should be considered as one among many if the appropriate assertions are to be made or conclusions drawn about the future. A diagnosis made from the birth chart alone might, with luck, be correct, but there is no guarantee of this.

If we consider the cosmic birth chart (cosmogram), to be a cosmic pattern of the tendencies within an individual, then we cannot say that this must have a particular effect but rather that it may, in certain circumstances, trigger it.

We believe that the tendencies created by the pattern found in the cosmogram can be affected at certain moments during a lifetime by transit or progression. Here, too, one must pay particular attention to the various possibilities created by diverse circumstances. One may, therefore, speak of possible developments or tendencies but never predict events precisely because one only knows the cosmic factors and not the other conditions prevailing at a given time. Predestination, or a predictable fate, can thus be rejected. This of course does not preclude the possibility of events being forecast, but one has to take into consideration the state and disposition of the circumstances in force at the time. We must therefore differentiate between the purely symbolic interpretation, or intuitive vision, and the recognition of a regular pattern of development.

The astrologer in ancient of medieval times engrossed himself in a horoscope and meditated upon it. The cosmobiologist of today, on the other hand, with the help of modern science tries to observe a pattern and conduct investigations from a firm base created by all the relevant facts. Both in earlier times and today many astrologers examine a horoscope in isolation and this is borne out by the examples we find in astrological literature. Cosmobiology, however, relates its investigations to those of other sciences. It may, for example, look for confirmation of the facts in graphology, a psychological test, or in medical case histories. It also relates the case under consideration to others found in its records, thus comparing it with the empirical knowledge found therein.

Cosmobiology does not believe in the stars but looks for a cosmic pattern and then confirms this with the help of other disciplines. It is striving for the development of astrology as a science in much the same way as the chemists created a science out of alchemy.

A Firm Base

Scientific work, and above all scientific cooperation, is only possible when a common and unified ground is agreed upon. Corruption in the world of astrology is caused by the use of multifarious and multilayered methods of interpretation. If one considers carefully the processes that have produced the greatest number of hits, or correct predictions, they are by no means as many or so different from the systems that use them. It is for this reason that the author advocates that in cooperative work the most important common methods should be used, and for the sake of unity, the less scientific, though customary systems, should be jettisoned.

For astrologers and cosmobiologists, the following form a universally acceptable base:

1. The positions of the stellar bodies in the zodiac.

2. The Midheaven and the Ascendant.

3. The angular relationship between the stellar bodies (aspects and midpoints).

For the purposes of prediction, that is the determination of the exact moment when a cosmic pattern is triggered, the following have proved themselves to be reliable:

1. The progressed aspects are calculated using the formula of one day equals one year of life. For example, for the thirtieth year

of life, one examines the aspects between the stellar bodies on the thirtieth day after birth (the birth date is the first year) with those in the birth chart. Further, suppose that the progressed Sun in that year forms a conjunction with natal Venus. This conjunction could indicate a love affair in the thirtieth year of the individual's life.

2. When the Sun's arc is used the stellar bodies are advanced according to the formula that one degree of the Sun's arc equals one year of life. The use of the Sun's arc in this way is known as the Naibod formula.

3. Transits are found by applying the current position of the stellar bodies, found from an ephemeris, to their positions in aspect to the birth chart.

With the aid of these basic methods almost every contingency experienced by man can be forecast and it thus is unnecessary to resort to such things as sensitive points, supposed planets, and any other astronomically unproven data. If an astrologer finds that he cannot achieve the results he requires without the aid of these unconfirmed systems, then he must accept the confusion that must inevitably ensue. Furthermore, one can only consider a study scientific if all the factors have been taken into consideration; one cannot just leave out certain elements because they do not fit into the scheme.

When carrying out a concentrated study of a birth chart and selecting the most important facts therefrom, it has been found that the use of the 90°-circle has been most helpful.

Reinhold Ebertin

Diagnosis

*T*he aim of a diagnosis is to assemble a comprehensive picture from a series of facts, draw the appropriate conclusions therefrom, and from this make a prediction.

A diagnostic delineation cannot deal with a cosmogram in its entirety and consider its every detail. It must instead rapidly select the most significant features and in particular those that are important to the development of the individual.

The diagnosis must be accurate and therefore reliable. In order to achieve this the prominent features of the birth chart cannot be considered in isolation but should be compared with other similar cases.

We must also state that by a proven prediction we are not referring to a general forecasting of the fate of an individual but rather to a specific area of enquiry because we have found that this kind of prediction is likely to be more accurate. Cosmobiological studies have been made of particular constellations such as Sun/Saturn and Moon/Saturn and these have served to confirm our view.

Let us now single out the effects of Sun/Saturn aspects. These were found to occur when there were developments due to illness, an early death of the parent, or difficulties in the environment. Statistical experience has proved that such a constellation does in fact create checks in the development of an individual; but if one tries to go further and forecast the kind of illness or the death of a parent, then the prediction may prove to be wrong.

In the same way the Moon/Saturn aspects were studied and revealed that with this constellation the relationship to the mother was poor, coupled with a tendency to stomach troubles. Further investigations showed that one could expect to find a limited emotional development as well as difficulties experienced in the sowing of emotion; but this was not always accompanied by a poor relationship with the mother or by stomach troubles. Of all the cases studied, about sixty-four percent lacked self-confidence, forty-two percent had a tendency to depression, thirty-one percent had a poor relationship with the mother (or an early death of the mother), and thirty-three percent had digestive troubles.

Because of the fact that in most cases there is a lack of statistical material to check against, one has to go to the cosmogram itself to ascertain the correctness of any prediction. In the case of a small child, one should look at the birth chart in conjunction with the birth charts of the parents. If one finds in this comparison that the child and the parents, or for that matter the grandparents, have in their birth charts a similar constellation, and they have suffered from a similar tendency to a given illness, then one may assume that the child is likely to have the same weakness. This weakness may, however, be offset if preventive steps are taken in time.

It should be noted, nevertheless, that inclinations to illness are likely only to show themselves late in life. I recently dealt with the case of a seventy-six year old woman whose husband was very worried about her illness. This illness was evident in certain precise aspects between the heavenly bodies situated in Leo (the heart) and in Scorpio in the birth chart, but the serious heart trouble from which she still suffers did not manifest until she was sixty years old.

The intention of a diagnostic delineation is therefore to identify the vital elements from a cosmogram and draw from them certain conclusions as to when the tendencies therein might make their appearance.

Reinhold Ebertin

Successful People

The charts of several successful people are good examples to illustrate the cosmobiological influences at work. Each is well known in his or her field of endeavor and recognized for various achievements.

Hans Porst (Photo-Porst)

The author discussed this chart at the Tenth Work Congress for Cosmobiological Research at Aalen (see Figure 1). The first question asked by members of that congress was: "Which is the most important constellation in the horoscope?" One can recognize immediately the Sun-Saturn square as an important aspect. With Saturn in the second house, it would naturally affect the financial status of the native and according to traditional astrology this position is interpreted as: "He rarely has a pocket full of money." A further prominent aspect is the close conjunction of Venus and Mars, which should affect the love and marriage status of the individual. Finally there is the Pluto-Neptune conjunction; however, this aspect lasts for several years and therefore, has only a minimal affect upon the character, provided no other factors combine with it. The factors we consider significant to the individual character are those that combine with the personal points: Sun, Moon, Ascendant, and Midheaven.

Jupiter is in the tenth house, which would traditionally signify success both in social position and career, but is has no connection with other elements in the horoscope. We must therefore accept that the Sun-Saturn square will be the most decisive configuration and have the most effect upon the native's life.

Everyone present agreed with this judgment. They were thus somewhat surprised when it was revealed that this was the chart of an exceptionally successful businessman who is well known internationally as Photo-Porst (Hans Porst), the owner of one of the largest photographic export businesses in the world, which has a turnover of many millions a year.

In order to compare different horoscopes, it is essential that the form in which they are presented be standardized. Up to the present, the Ascendant has been placed horizontally, while the Midheaven has had the vertical position. The signs of the zodiac were then placed in their correct positions around the circle. In this way a horoscope can be better understood, for it symbolizes the correct position of the stellar bodies in space.

However, for scientific comparison it is essential that the basic elements of the horoscope appear in a uniform position. The advantages of such a procedure will become evident if one examines each month a series of cosmograms of the leading political figures and pays particular attention to the aspects formed by the transits.

Figure 1 shows today's traditional horoscope presentation. The division of houses is shown, as are the planetary placements.

However, as a result of our investigations we use the zodiac as a means of classification and as a measuring circle. Because the Sun reaches its zenith at 0 Cancer, it is therefore obvious that it must be placed at the top of the chart. In order to obtain an overall picture and to facilitate and quicken understanding of the different combinations, a 90°-degree circle is placed around the outside of the 360°-circle; this is of practical help when comparing examples.

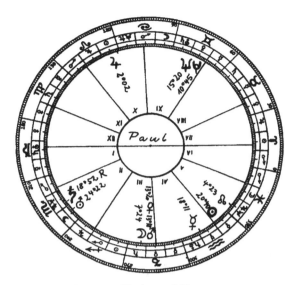

Figure 1. Traditional Horoscope.

Let us now consider Figure 2 (see page 14) as a means of explaining the 90°-circle. The inside shows the natal chart in its traditional. Outside of the chart are written the same planets but in a 90°-placement. For example, the Moon at 7 Capricorn is in the upper left hand corner on the outside of the chart. This is because the segment 0-30° contains the cardinal signs: Aries, Cancer, Libra, and Capricorn. The Midheaven is thus placed close to the Moon, in the fifteen-degree position because it is also in a cardinal sign (Cancer) and therefore belongs to the same group.

Having completed this process, one can see at a glance that in the upper left hand corner outside the traditional natal chart is the Moon, the Ascendant, Mars, Venus, and the Midheaven. These are all found together in some cases due to their conjunction and in others due to their opposition.

At the bottom right of the outside circle we have Mercury and Saturn, and Sun and Uranus, which are all in close proximity because they are all in fixed signs (Scorpio and Aquarius). These

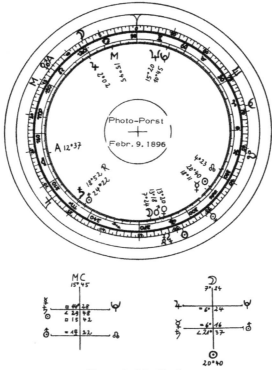

Figure 2. 90°-Circle.

are thus allocated to the 30-60° segment of the circle.

From this we can see that there are two areas of the 90°-circle which are emphasized, firstly 7-15° and then 48-55°. One of the primary aims of our research is the understanding of such emphasized areas. It is also important to know which are the prominent aspects and whether they are exact, or very close, or in a wide orb, and how long will it take them to become effective.

We are mainly interested in the relationship between the Sun and Saturn. Looking at the ephemeris for the year 1896, which was the year of his birth, we find that Saturn moved slowly forward until on the twentieth day after birth it began to turn retrograde. It never reached the degree in which it would form an exact square to the Sun. This causes the inhibiting aspect to become impotent. The author does not know whether this Sun-Saturn connection has caused any illness, but it has by no means hindered the native's progress in life.

In order to fully come to terms with the condition of a planet within the cosmogram, one has to examine the many correlations that comprise its cosmic status. Because the Sun or Saturn in different birth charts varies in position, the final interpretation will depend upon its relationship to the whole chart.

For such investigations the 90°-dial is a great help. The chart in 90°-dial form can be calculated using astrological software. Used in such a way that the arrow points to the Sun, then it can be seen that on the one side Uranus and on the other Mercury are equidistant from the arrow and the line of the arrow forms the axis. The picture looks like this:

Sun

Uranus   Mercury/Saturn

Furthermore, it can be seen that Jupiter and Pluto are equidistant from the arrow. If one follows the line of the axis away from the arrow head, one will find the Moon is at the end. We can therefore, complete the picture as follows:

Pluto   Jupiter

Moon

By doing this we have established the cosmic picture of the Sun. All these investigations are carried out on the 90°-dial and we only need to look at the 360°-circle to confirm the relationship and the overall picture. The distance from the axis is considered equal provided it does not differ by more than one and a half degrees. If one wishes to prove these midpoints to a greater degree of accuracy it will be necessary to calculate the midpoint between the two factors. This can be done by using either the 360°- or the 90°-circle. In both cases one counts the number of degrees between 0 Aries and the factor's position. In our example of Jupiter and Pluto we get the following:

	360°	*90°*
Jupiter 20°02' Leo =	122°02'	32°02'
Pluto 10°45' Gemini =	70°45'	70°45'
Jupiter/Pluto =	192°47'	102°47'
Midpoint Jupiter/Pluto =	96°23'	51°23'

96°23' is 6°23' Cancer

51°23' is 21°23' Taurus, Leo, Scorpio, Aquarius

It would seem from this that these two results are not the same, but if we refer to the 360° circle one can see that there is a distance of 45° between the two factors. As with the 90°-dial we calculate throughout with angles that are multiples of 45°. The Moon at 7 Cancer 42 is within one degree of the center of the Jupiter/Pluto axis. The Moon is also in a 45°-aspect to the Sun, which is at 20 Aquarius 46. The calculations for Mercury/Uranus would be the same.

If one examines all the factors in the same way one arrives at the cosmic structures as shown in Figure 3. When studying these cosmic structures we can see immediately that there are certain elements that continuously recur:

Sun = Jupiter /Pluto	Exceptional success
Moon = Jupiter/Pluto	A mass effect
Midheaven = Sun/Pluto	Powerful drives
Ascendant = Sun/Pluto	Self-assertion
Venus = Mercury/Pluto	Interest in art
Mars = Mercury/Pluto	Indefatigable
Pluto = Jupiter/Midheaven	A successful person

The above interpretations are from *The Combination of Stellar Influences* by the author.

In order to complete the picture it might prove useful to set out one of these cosmic structures in its entirety without the aspects.

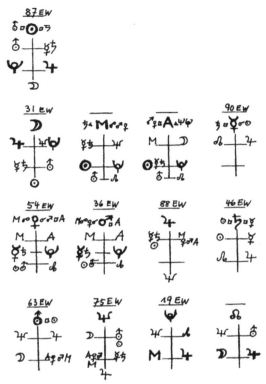

Figure 3. Cosmic Structure Pattern for Hans Porst's Birth Chart.

Midheaven = Mercury/Pluto: The ability to cope with any situation. Good powers of observation. Keen power of judgment. The ability to arrange matters well.

Midheaven = Saturn/Pluto: To rise from difficult circumstances through the application of tenacity and endurance.

Midheaven = Sun/Pluto: A striving for power, consciousness of purpose or objective, qualities of leadership.

Midheaven = Uranus/Node: A desire for change and variety for one's own benefit. The tendency to seek stimulating ideas from and through other people.

The aim of cosmobiological diagnosis is to be able to understand the relationship between the ability of the individual and the actual course of his life. It is of course valuable to be able to recognize a person's ability, but it is of even greater use to be able to tell exactly when these abilities are likely to manifest and assert an influence upon the individual's life pattern.

After having examined the birth chart, we must now take the ephemeris for 1896 and examine the movements of the planets for that year in relation to the birth chart. We have already noted the important interrelationship between the Sun, Saturn, Mercury, and Uranus on the one hand, and the Moon, Ascendant, Mars, Venus, and Midheaven on the other. It will be of particular interest to see how these develop.

Until February 28, 1896, the nineteenth day after birth, which corresponds to the nineteenth year of life, Saturn moved to 19 Scorpio 07, i.e., toward Saturn square Sun, before turning retrograde. From this we gather that the inhibitions in development associated with the Sun-Saturn square have partially been overcome. Between February 24 and 29, Saturn was at 19 Scorpio 17, and then turned retrograde, moving at one degree per day/ year by solar arc. It is difficult, because it is so small, to see the effect of a one degree movement in the life of the individual. The native was nineteen years old in 1915, and this coincided with the period of the Great War. It is, therefore, obvious that he was hardly in a position to start any "great enterprise," which would be indicated by the cosmic structures operative at that time.

On March 2, 1896 (the native was then twenty-two years old, and the year was 1918), we find progressed Venus trine Pluto. On March 5, 1896 (age twenty five, 1921), we find progressed Mars at 1 Aquarius 30 and it came exactly into opposition with Jupiter, while at the same time progressed Mercury at 18 Aquarius came into conjunction with natal Mercury and a square to natal Saturn. These constellations seem to be indicative of vocational development.

The aspects created by progression could also be checked by using the solar arc method (moving all factors one degree for each year of life). Looking at a 90° chart, we can examine the period between the twentieth and twenty-fifth years of life, and discover that the natal Moon's position is 25° from Jupiter (see Figure 4), indicating the twenty-fifth year of life.

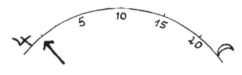

Figure 4.

Similarly, we will find that there is a distance of 20° between the Ascendant-Mars-Venus group and Jupiter, which corresponds to the twentieth year of life, or 1916, which was about the middle of the Great War.

If we look past Jupiter, we find that between Jupiter and Uranus there are between 22° and 23° and this in turn would indicate a period between the twenty-second and twenty-third year of life.

By advancing the Sun 20° we find that it reaches Pluto, and if we do the same with Mercury and Saturn we find that they too group with Pluto. If we advance Uranus 20°, then it reaches Neptune, and if we move Neptune 22° it reaches the Moon. We can, therefore summarize as follows the most important groups shown in Figure 5:

- February 28, 1896, age 19, 1915, Saturn turns retrograde
- February 29, 1896, age 20, 1916, Mars, Ascendant, Venus advanced to Jupiter; Sun advanced to Pluto
- March 1, 1896, age 21, 1917, - - -
- March 2, 1896, age 22, 1918, progressed Venus trine Pluto, Neptune advanced to Moon, Saturn advanced to Pluto, Mercury advanced to Pluto

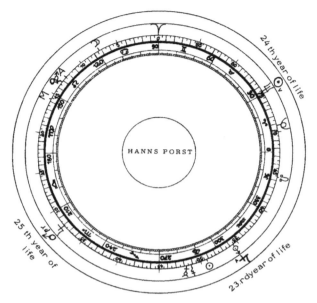

Figure 5. Age 23 = 1919, Jupiter advanced to Uranus; Age 24 = 1920, Sun advanced to Neptune; Age 25 = 1921, Mars progressed to Jupiter.

- March 3, 1896, age 23, 1919, Jupiter advanced to Uranus

- March 4, 1896, age 24, 1920, Sun advanced to Neptune

- March 5, 1896, age 25, 1921, progressed Mars, Jupiter, Moon advanced to Jupiter; progressed Sun trine Midheaven

- March 6, 1896, age 26, 1922, progressed Sun sesquisquare Jupiter

From all this it is quite easy to recognize that between 1919 and 1921, there should be an important turning point in the native's career as indicated by the positions of the cosmic factors. One must always have the cosmic structures of the birth chart in mind and at the same time recognize the effect on the conditions of these structures created by the progression and advancement of the factors. In a way the advancing factors release or trigger

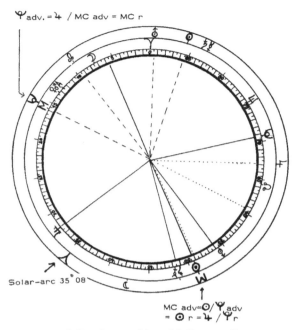

Ψadv. = ♃ / MC adv = MC r

Solar-arc 35° 08´

MC adv=☉/Ψadv
= ☉ r = ♃ /Ψ r

Figure 6. Sun-Jupiter-Pluto-Midheaven Contacts.

the cosmic structures of the birth chart, but this does not happen with the progressed positions as these have to be examined as a separate entity and interpreted as such.

With Jupiter advancing we can take the following elements as positive:

> Jupiter = Mercury/Sun
>
> Jupiter = Sun/Mars
>
> Jupiter = Sun/Midheaven
>
> Jupiter = Mercury/Ascendant
>
> Jupiter = Mercury/Mars
>
> Jupiter = Sun/Ascendant

and as negative:

> Jupiter = Saturn/Midheaven

Jupiter = Saturn/ Ascendant
Jupiter = Saturn/Venus
Jupiter = Saturn/Mars

It will be found that like Jupiter, Uranus has more positive midpoints than negative, which will indicate a favorable change at this time of life. Through progressed Mars and Moon advancing to Jupiter is once again stimulated and this increases its effect. The Moon and the Sun form the axis of the midpoint Jupiter/Pluto. We should remember that the cosmic structure Midheaven = Sun/Pluto was in the birth chart. There should, therefore, be some relationship between the Midheaven and Pluto, which is indeed the case (see Figure 6). Pluto advancing 35° to reach the Midheaven would result in the following:

Midheaven = Sun/Pluto advanced	Powerful drives
Natal Sun = Jupiter/Pluto	Exceptional success
Pluto advanced = Jupiter/Midheaven	A successful person
Natal Midheaven = natal Sun/Pluto	As above

These are the influences that in Hans Porst's cosmogram correlate with a profit of 3.5 million marks in 1931. He began his business just after the Great War with an investment of 600 gold marks.

The examples taken from this case have been kept as simple as possible so they can be easily understood by the reader. The cosmobiological diagnosis would therefore be as follows:

> The cosmic structures in Hans Porst's cosmogram indicate a period of great success. This is particularly exhibited by the cosmic activity of the Sun, Moon, Midheaven, Ascendant, and Pluto. There are two important groupings in this cosmogram: Mercury-Saturn-Sun-Uranus-(Moon), and Venus-Mars-Ascendant-Midheaven. The trend toward success could be activated if these groupings relate to one another or with other configurations. The Sun-Saturn square is

unlikely to become effective because Saturn turns retrograde. This aspect may be operative up to the nineteenth year of life, but after this he can count upon more favorable conditions. There is a possibility for exceptional success when Jupiter advanced is square Uranus, progressed Mars is opposition Jupiter; and Moon advanced is opposition Jupiter; this could occur between the twenty-third and twenty-fifth year of his life, those years being 1919-1921. It was during that time that he founded his business.

A second favorable period should occur about age thirty-five (Figure 6). The cosmic conditions giving rise to this are: Midheaven advanced to Sun and Pluto advanced to Midheaven. At this time the cosmic structure Midheaven = Sun/Pluto found in the birth chart was activated twice, and reached its peak effectiveness about 1931.

Having completed our first example in detail it would seem appropriate that we should cite further illustrations based upon similar groupings, but this we can do in a shortened form. In this way we can confirm our methods. It should be made clear, however, that when one finds influences in the birth chart that indicate success, they will denote only the prosperity itself and not the means through which it comes. Thus achievement in this case can be attained in the clerical, organizational, vocational, or sporting fields, but this will be indicated by influences other than those that point to the success itself.

Arturo Toscanini

This celebrated Italian conductor was known for his perfectionism and photographic memory. He served as music director at La Scala, Metropolitan Opera, and New York Philharmonic Orchestra. He was later the first music director of the NBC Symphony Orchestra. His birth time was rectified by the author.

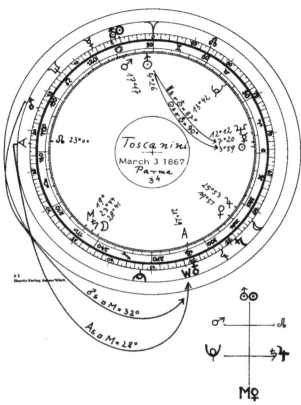

Figure 7. Arturo Toscanini

On the 90° version of the cosmogram (Figure 7) we find two groupings that oppose each other: Ascendant-Mars-Mercury-Sun-Uranus is in opposition to Pluto-Midheaven-Venus-Jupiter-Saturn-Moon. Following our previous example we can see at once the following planetary picture:

Sun/Uranus

Mars   Node

Pluto   Jupiter/Saturn

Midheaven/Venus

            Reinhold Ebertin

Interpreting this we get something like the following: an extraordinary and magical use of energy (he was often called the "magician of the baton"), ambition, assiduousness, organizational talent, managerial success, a cooperative attitude, and great success. When then will this planetary picture first become evident in his life? If one makes a survey of this cosmogram, one will see that the Ascendant and Mars are moving toward the group in the birth chart. The distance between the Ascendant and Midheaven/Venus is approximately 28° and from Mars to Midheaven/Venus is 32°.

His biography offers confirmation of his success. Arturo Toscanini was the son of a tailor who was given the opportunity to study at the Conservatoire, where he passed his examinations with honors. In the beginning he was only able to earn his living as a stand-in cellist in theater orchestras. In the spring of 1896, when he was age twenty-nine, he had to take over the baton from the conductor, who was unable to be present, at a performance of Aida in Rio de Janeiro; this brought him considerable acclaim. After that he traveled around Italy, formed a choir and orchestra, and then at age 31, he was named musical director at La Scala. He reorganized and turned La Scala into a unique artistic center.

In using cosmobiology in diagnosis one finds that the difference of one year is unimportant provided one knows the approximate timing for the triggering of the main influences in the birth chart; this then confirms the abilities found therein. One must realize that the cosmogram is not an inflexible structure, but that there is life within it which will only manifest when there is a correlation between the birth chart and a releasing agent.

The same influence was again activated when he was age eighty-seven (Mercury/Uranus) and gave his last concert, and again at the time of his death, when he was age 90, at which time the Sun advanced to Uranus.

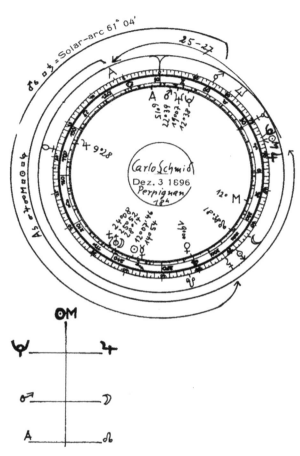

Figure 8. Carlo Schmid.

Carlo Schmid

This is another case of Midheaven = Jupiter/Pluto. We asked for his Carlo Schmid's birth certificate and found that it states that he was born at 6:00 pm, March 12, 1896 at Perpignan in the South of France (Figure 8). In addition to the Midheaven, we also find that the Sun = Jupiter/Pluto. At about age twenty-five this constellation reached his Ascendant, and it was during that time that he established himself as a legal counselor in Tubingen. He was named a judge and advisor to the Wurtemburg Institute of Public and International Law. He lectured on international law at the University of Tubingen in 1929 and soon afterwards was to join the International Court of Settlements. If the Ascendant is advanced about sixty-four years it will be found to rest above the previously mentioned constellation, and it will therefore be interesting to see what role he will play in the government. One has to consider how his health will stand up to the demands made upon it, as in November 1956, when Mars was square Saturn, he had a heart attack from which he has apparently made an excellent recovery.

Eva Kotthaus

Eva Kotthaus gave her birth data as May 19, 1932, 10:45 pm, Dusseldorf, Germany (see Figure 9 on page 28).

Here the Midheaven = Jupiter /Pluto is found again, but in a different profession—acting. Eva had to overcome many difficulties prior to being discovered by Helmut Kautner, including living behind the iron curtain. For her performance in the "Himmel ohne Sterne" (The Sky Without Stars), she received an Oscar at the Gloria Palast in Berlin on June 22, 1956.

Looking at the cosmogram, it is not difficult to see the constellation of Mercury, Mars, and Saturn retrograde. There is, therefore, a Mercury/Mars square to Saturn, but this will probably not become exact because Saturn is retrograde and so will not have its full effect; nevertheless, it will for some decades move toward the Midheaven. Bearing in mind the previous example, it should not be too difficult to see on the 90°-dial that the Midheaven is in the center of Jupiter/Pluto. Examining the two sides of the cosmogram, we find that the Moon and Venus are opposite each other. An angle of 135° (sesquisquare) is involved here and at the center of the Midheaven, which forms an angle of 45° (semisquare). We therefore get Midheaven = Moon/Venus.

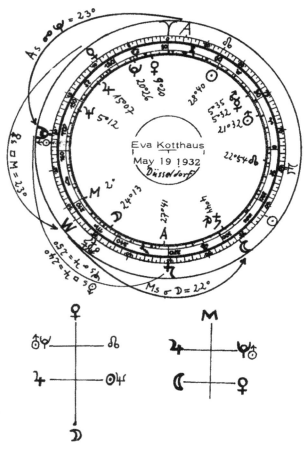

Figure 9. Eva Kotthaus.

Now observe the combinations when she was about age twenty-four: Ascendant advanced to conjunct Pluto (age twenty-three), Venus advanced to square Midheaven (age twenty-three), Midheaven advanced to conjunct Moon (age twenty-two), Uranus advanced to square Jupiter (age twenty-four), and Pluto advanced to conjunct Jupiter (age twenty-five). Her great success was achieved when she was age twenty-five, and little was heard of her in the film world after that. It is of particular interest to compare her life with that of Lili Palmer and Horst Bucholz, both of whom received an Oscar at the same time as Eva.

Fritz Sanger

This example shows that despite the fact that we do not know his birth time, we can confirm the correlation between the native's life and the grouping of the heavenly bodies. Fritz Sanger was born December 24, 1901 in Stettin, Germany (see Figure 10 on page 30). First a school master, later he turned to journalism and became editor-secretary of the German Civil Servants Union, then manager of the Teacher's Association, and in 1932 was named editor of the association's newspaper. He lost his position when the National Socialists were in power and remained without work for several years. In 1935 he was employed by the *Frankfurter Zeitung* newspaper. His rise to prominence came after the capitulation, when he was appointed commissioner and given the task of building up the Socialist Press, which later became the Deutsche Presse-Agentur news agency. This organization supplied the German and foreign press with news and information. He was also a member of many state and public organizations, reaching a key position in the press industry.

A first look at the cosmogram does not appear to give us the picture of a successful person. Jupiter conjunct Mars points to success, but Jupiter conjunct Saturn indicates great difficulty. Neptune opposition Sun cannot be said to be helpful. Venus trine Pluto and semisquare Sun might be considered as positive.

On the 90°-dial, the combination Sun/Neptune stands out. The opposition of Uranus/Pluto, which will last for several years, has no special significance. Moon conjunct Pluto could be of significance, but its exactitude is unknown as we are ignorant of the birth time.

It will be noted by the experienced astrologer that the Sun in opposition to Venus falls on the midpoint and forms the axis of

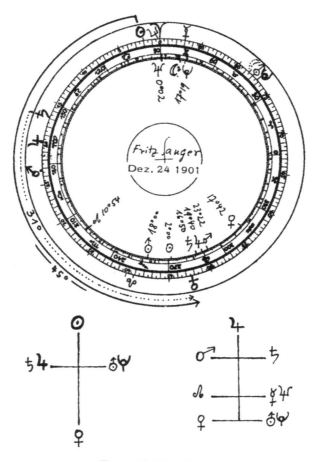

Figure 10. Fritz Sanger

Uranus/Pluto on the one side and Jupiter/Saturn on the other. This is in contrast to the previous examples we have quoted, where the Midheaven was at the midpoint of Jupiter/Pluto; here, the Sun takes up that position.

Fritz Sanger, according to his biography, experienced a considerable rise in fortune when he was age thirty. The complete picture can be seen if we study the following constellations: the Pluto/

Reinhold Ebertin

Sun complex (approximately age fifteen); Sun/Jupiter (ages fifteen to twenty-one); Jupiter/Venus with Sun in axis (ages twenty-five to thirty-one); Pluto/Jupiter (ages thirty to thirty-five); and Sun/Venus (approximately age forty-five). The distance between Mars and Venus resulted in activity when he was about age twenty-five, but one should remember that Venus is in the axis of the Sun so that not only Venus but also Sun = Jupiter/Pluto became operative.

At about age thirty-one, advanced Saturn conjoined natal Venus, indicating a negative discharge. At that time Fritz Sanger lost his job, but one must also take into consideration the conditions operative at that time. Hitler came to power when Jupiter came into relationship with Uranus/Pluto and this was not helped by a Mars/Saturn contact.

His most successful period came when he was about age forty-five. The Sun had by then reached Venus and this caused an activation of the whole of the Sun axis. Here, we also have to consider the external circumstances. At this time leaders were needed, especially in the press, which had suffered under the Nazi regime. Sanger must have undergone another crisis in the spring of 1959, because a short time later the press gave the news that he had left the Deutsche Presse-Agentur. We can find a correspondence in his stellar pattern that coincides with this because the Jupiter group moved toward the Pluto constellation. When Jupiter advanced by 58° it formed a square to Pluto.

Herbert Von Karajan

Orchestral conductor Herbert Von Karajan was born at 10:30 pm on April 5, 1908, in Salzburg, Germany (see Figure 11 on page 32). He has been peculiarly successful in his career. After finishing his studies he was appointed stage musical director to the Salzburg Festival. From 1928 (age twenty) to 1933, he was musical director of the theater in Ulm. In 1934, he was asked to take over the position of assistant director of the opera at Aachen, and in 1935, he succeeded Peter Raabe as musical di-

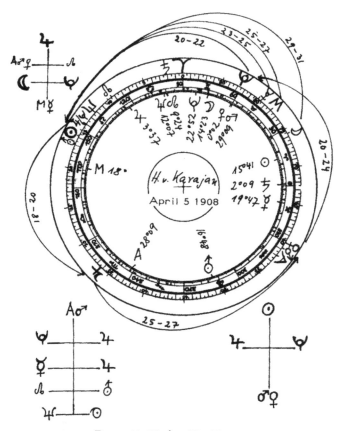

Figure 11. Herbert Von Karajan.

rector. In the autumn of 1938 he had his first success as a guest conductor at the Berlin State Opera. This was followed by a permanent engagement.

The midpoint of Jupiter/Pluto is 13 Cancer 15 and around it can be found the Sun, Venus, Mars, and the Ascendant. This constellation interacts, as can be seen in Figure 11. Prominence is given to Jupiter = Moon/Pluto = Mercury/Midheaven, which became operative between the eighteenth and thirty-first year of his life.

Reinhold Ebertin

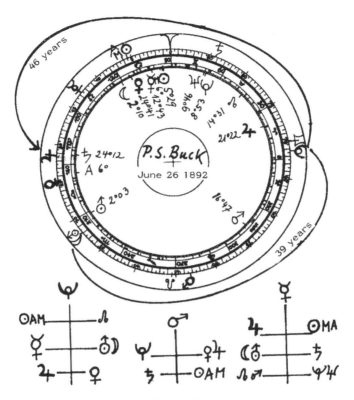

Figure 12. Pearl S. Buck.

Pearl S. Buck

Pearl Buck is considered by many as one of the most successful writers and this is corroborated by the large number of books she wrote. She was born at 12:30 pm on the June 26, 1892, at Hillsboro, West Virginia (Figure 12). The daughter of a missionary who was stationed in China, she was educated both in Europe and the United States and obtained several degrees. Because of her mother's illness she returned to Nanking in 1914, where she married John Lossing Buck, a professor at the local university, in 1917. After the publication of her first novel, *East Wind West Wind*, in 1929, she had enormous success with *The Good Earth* in 1931, for which she was given the Nobel Prize for Literature in 1938.

In the cosmogram there are several characteristic groupings: Sun-Midheaven-Ascendant, Jupiter-Venus, Moon-Uranus, Mars-Node, Neptune-Pluto. On the 90°-dial the main structure of the birth chart is emphasized. Not much experience is needed to recognize the main planetary formation:

Ascendant-Midheaven-Sun

Jupiter   Pluto-Neptune

Node-Mars

The axis Ascendant-Midheaven-Sun is not exactly opposite Node-Mars so that one must examine it separately. We cannot go into all the details of each birth chart here, but have to extract certain constellations for special study. From these we can draw conclusions:

Mars = Jupiter/Pluto	The desire to achieve great things.
Moon = Uranus = Mars/Jupiter	A successful woman. Ambition, resolution recognition.
Mercury = Sun/ Jupiter	Success through thought, discussion and commerce.
Mercury = Jupiter/Midheaven	A wealth of thought. Prudence, farsightedness. Successful plans. Good business associations.
Mercury = Jupiter/Ascendant	Exchange of suggestions. Stimulating ideas. Exchange of thoughts.
Mercury = Mars/Pluto	An energetic realization of plans.

Pluto = Moon/Mercury	A realization of tragedy.
Pluto = Mercury/Uranus	Sudden realization of plans.
Pluto = Venus/Jupiter	The enjoyment of an unusual amount of popularity.

In this cosmogram we can again see when and how an aspect becomes active. Jupiter was moving toward a square with Venus, and it reached it by progression within four minutes of the time of publication of her first successful novel, in 1931. Progressed Jupiter at 24 Aries 45 (age thirty-nine) was square Venus at 24 Cancer 41 (= Pluto = Sun/Mars, = Mars/Ascendant = Mars/Midheaven = Moon/Jupiter, etc.). This constellation had a steadying influence because Jupiter was stationary at 24 Aries 56 and this held the exact square to Venus for decades.

It should also be noted that at about age thirty-nine, progressed Mercury at 8 Virgo 43 was square Pluto. When she received the Nobel Prize, Pluto was at 22 Cancer 33 and transited the square to Jupiter; it was also moving toward the conjunction with Venus.

She also wrote several novels with an American background under the *nom de plume* of John Sedges, which only goes to show that she was good enough to obtain mass circulation even under another name.

Change and Transformation

*I*t is not often that life moves along in the way one expects, or in the way that educators have predicted. A particular experience, a sickness, a discovery, or a sudden revelation can suddenly alter one's whole destiny. The following cases will show how the course of life can abruptly alter its aim.

Max Bircher-Benner

Max Bircher-Benner was born during the night of the August 22, 1867 (see Figure 13 on page 38). He was a seven-month baby with a cardiac weakness, and his delicate condition necessitated a toughening of the physical body, which later became the impetus in the development of his medical career.

The birth is supposed to have occurred at 2:30 am, but even if we do not accept this birth time as correct we still have several constellations that indicate very little success in life. Saturn is in opposition to the Moon and square Venus, which would denote difficulties in life as well as bad health. Mars square Uranus marks him as a revolutionary and this he demonstrated in his actions to alter medical thought and set it upon a new foundation. That sudden outburst of energy supplied by Mars and Uranus

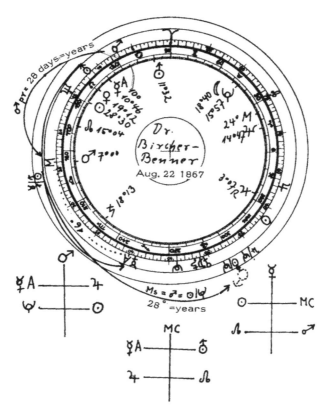

Figure 13. Max Bircher-Benner

seems to be the central core around which his life developed.

On the 90°-dial, one can immediately see three constellations: Mars-Uranus-Neptune, Ascendant-Mercury-Pluto-Saturn-Moon-Venus, and Sun-Jupiter. The axis of Mars/Uranus falls in the center of all the other constellations. Taking into consideration what we have said before, Mars = Jupiter/Pluto = Mercury/Pluto = Sun/Pluto is of importance.

A powerful change of thought is indicated by Uranus advanced to a conjunction with Mercury in his twenty-eighth year, when progressed Mars came into opposition with the Midheaven (if the birth time is correct) and exactly square Mercury/Uranus. This denotes a quick recognition of any situation, the understanding of complicated correlations, and the development of resolute action. If the Midheaven is correct and it were advanced twenty-eight years it would be in the axis of Jupiter/ Pluto. That Bircher-Benner had difficulty in succeeding in a breakthrough because he was an outsider is not difficult to see. But when in 1900, his lecture to the Zurich physicians was headlined in the newspaper as "Dr. Bircher-Benner has left the frontiers of Science," it is strange to note that ten years later he was hailed as "The Father of a new doctrine in nutrition."

In view of this illustration it is interesting to advance the Midheaven some 16° (sixteen years). In the first instance Mercury was reached, indicating a profound self-knowledge and a stabilizing clear and objective aim in life. Then follows the Midheaven coming into conjunction with Pluto. This constellation has been repeatedly recognized as the symbol of an inner change, and an inclination to look upon one's profession as a calling or mission. In order to reach his aim he had to go through an opposition of the Midheaven to Saturn and a conjunction with the Moon; after that, his way was clear. After moving 28°, the Midheaven was within only a few degrees of the midpoint Sun/Mercury, which denotes a development of his own concepts and convictions, and Sun/Pluto (ambition, industry and success). Together these constellations coincide with Uranus reaching Mercury.

Karl Jaspers

Karl Jaspers was originally a physician, starting as an assistant in the psychiatric clinic at the University of Heidelberg; he was confirmed in the post in 1913, and nominated for a professorship in 1916. Shortly after that Karl Jaspers changed to philosophy and in 1919 published his *The Psychology of the Conception of Life*. He then became professor extraordinarius at the same university and in the following year was named professor ordinarius. Jaspers was born February 2, 1883 at 2:30 pm at Oldenburg, Germany (Figure 14).

When we look at his cosmogram, Uranus-Moon-Jupiter stands out, while on the opposite side Mercury and the Ascendant complete this axis which is found in the center of Sun/Midheaven. The Midheaven reaching Mercury indicated an onset of self-knowledge from which further development could be expected. The distance between the Midheaven and Mercury is about 27°, which corresponds to age twenty-seven. It was at that time that he was an assistant at the psychiatric clinic.

It was also then that the whole of this constellation was released, and this included the following basic patterns: the formation of one's personality and the storing up of experience (Midheaven = Mercury = Sun/Midheaven); psychic influences change one's aim in life (Uranus = Sun/Midheaven); and a clear and positive development of one's aim in life (Jupiter = Sun/Midheaven). The inner recognition of this change was followed by practical implementation after a few years had passed.

The Midheaven reached Mars and Neptune after a forward move of 34°, which was about 1917, and at this time he changed from psychiatry to philosophy. It should be noted that Mars/Neptune is almost in the center of Mercury/Saturn. Mercury/Saturn is considered to indicate a thinker or a philosopher and therefore the Midheaven passing over this constellation can be interpreted as:

I (Midheaven) am a philosopher (Mercury/Saturn).

Making an overall survey we can see that Mars/Neptune falls in the axis of the Midheaven on the left and the constellation of Uranus/Moon/Jupiter on the right, and we can therefore construct the following planetary picture:

Neptune = Mars = Uranus/Midheaven   Inspiration, perception, sudden realization.

Reinhold Ebertin

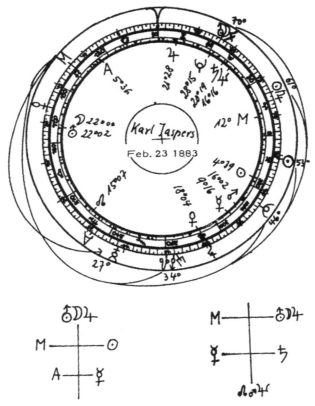

Figure 14. Karl Jaspers.

Neptune = Mars = Moon/Midheaven	Out of the unclear (Neptune) and into the clear (Mars). The attainment of psychological adjustment (Moon/Midheaven).
Neptune = Mars = Jupiter/Midheaven	The successful transferring of ideas and plans into action.

If there were any difficulties around 1921, due to the Midheaven passing over Saturn, these are unknown to the author. In about 1929, the Midheaven advanced had reached Pluto. Jaspers had shortly before this refused a transfer to Bonn. The Midheaven advanced/Pluto took on a negative quality because Pluto is in the axis of Sun/Saturn. At 53° the Midheaven advanced to a square to Saturn and this relates to the year 1936. If one examines the position of the Sun in the axis of Uranus-Moon-Jupiter on the one hand and Saturn on the other, one can only conclude that the following is likely to occur: A change or separation (Jupiter/Saturn); loneliness (Moon/Saturn); resistance, a lack of the ability to compromise; conditions of scorn, separation (Saturn/Uranus). These indications are confirmed in life by his dismissal from office in 1937, when the Nazis were in power.

If we move the Midheaven farther we do not reach another midpoint until Sun/Jupiter. The axis of this midpoint falls at 28 Aries. The semisquare was then in 13 Gemini. This point was reached by the Midheaven after an advance of 61°, when he was about age sixty-one (1944). In 1945, Jaspers was reinstated to his teaching post; Midheaven advanced = Sun/Jupiter denotes both his recognition and joy.

Mercury (in combination with Ascendant-Mercury-Jupiter-Moon-Uranus) reached the Midheaven after an advance of 57°. The Midheaven then moved toward the constellation Jupiter-Moon-Uranus, which was reached after a move of 70°; this related to the many honors he received at that time. It is also remarkable that at this period his religious (Jupiter) moods (Moon) also appeared. Jaspers then opposed the efforts of Rudolf Bultmann to remove the mythology from Christian teachings.

This example has shown us how the most important constellations in the cosmogram indicate the unfolding of life and how they influence it. Having followed the first half of life in this way, one can, by taking into consideration the time element, investigate the future trends in the same manner.

Reinhold Ebertin

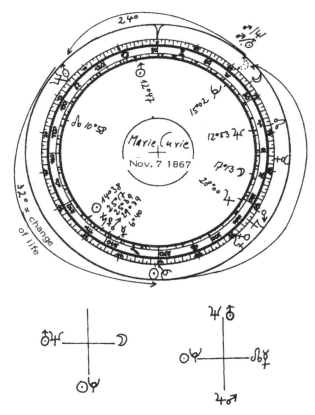

Figure 15. Marie Curie

Marie Curie

Marie Curie was born July 11, 1867 in Warsaw, Poland. In 1940, Heinz Noesselt, in an article in Sterne und Mensch, rectified her birth time to 1:24 pm (Figure 15).

There are two prominent constellations in this cosmogram: Uranus/Neptune opposition, Jupiter/Mars, and the Sun/Pluto combination. With reference to our previous investigations, it is interesting to discover what lies in the gap between Uranus-Neptune and Sun-Pluto. We can establish that the axis around which Neptune-Uranus-Mars-Jupiter are grouped lies between Mercury/Pluto and Sun/Mercury. Practical and mental abilities come together, imagination is condensed into fundamental knowledge, and there is a single-minded pursuit of her aim, leading to success and universal recognition.

All this happened around age thirty-two because Uranus advanced 32° and arrived at the square to Pluto; this then gave Uranus = Sun/Pluto, and Mars/Jupiter is added to this combination. This constellation indicated great knowledge and change, not only in her life but also for all humanity. Therefore, it was the birth of a new era.

On April 12, 1898, Marie Curie established the fact that the combination of Pitchblend and Uranium Cuprite emitted a greater radioactivity than Uranium alone, and that when these two were combined they produced a substance more powerfully radioactive than Uranium. At the end of 1898, the first news of this reached the public and many of the previously held conceptions of matter had to be reformulated. Radium had been discovered. In 1903, Marie Curie and her husband received the Nobel Prize for Chemistry. After the death of her husband, she became a professor at the Sorbonne in Paris, and director of the Radium Institute. Prior to all this, she had been obliged to work in a miserable shack and under the most primitive conditions.

By advancing Sun/Pluto 32°, it reached the Moon, which is also the midpoint between Mars/Uranus and Jupiter/Uranus. This singular combination translated into our cosmic language gives us: the desire to achieve something unusual, active intuition, circumspection, farsightedness, and the wish fulfilment of a woman. These circumstances are triggered by the Sun advanced as well as Pluto advanced, which gives us: an unusual desire for knowledge, strong consciousness of aim, much luck, and sudden changes for the better in financial matters.

The probable position of the Moon in the birth chart could be confirmed by the following: if you advance the Moon approxi-

Reinhold Ebertin

mately twenty-four years it comes into conjunction with Neptune and square to Uranus. At that time there was a great change in her life, and this manifested as her voyage from Warsaw to Paris.

Reinhold Ebertin

Dangerous Lives

There are people who do not value their lives, particularly if they are not given an opportunity to prove their courage and strength and to overcome dangers. They seldom remember the saying, "Those who seek danger may perish by it." The question therefore arises as to whether it is possible to foresee moments of danger.

Hermann Buhl

In 1953, Hermann Buhl conquered the Nanga Parbat, the ninth highest mountain in the world, but the ascent of this broad peak did not satisfy him. He still wanted to climb the fabulous, beautiful, powerful, and shining Baltoro. On June 27, 1957, he fell while ascending the Chogolisa. Hermann Buhl was born September 9, 1924, at 3:45 am in Innsbruck, Austria (see Figure 16 on page 48).

Looking at his cosmogram, we can see a peculiar planetary picture in which the Sun and Moon are in the axis. The combination of Jupiter/Pluto and Mercury/Pluto indicates unusual success, but the combination with Mars/Saturn denotes, besides success, that death may be lurking. As we have shown in previous examples, such planetary constellations are often activated by themselves when one of their members passes over another. In this case one exceptional danger must be recognized, and that

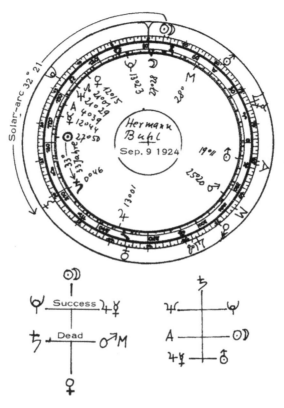

Figure 16. Hermann Buhl.

is when the advanced Sun and Moon position over Saturn. The distance from the Sun to Saturn is 33°. If we add thirty-three years to his year of birth we reach 1957, and this was the year of his death.

Bernd Rosemeyer

Bernd Rosemeyer was born October 14, 1909 at 9:10 am in Lingen, Germany (Figure 17). In this case the cosmogram is a picture of danger, with a cross of Neptune-Mercury and Sun-

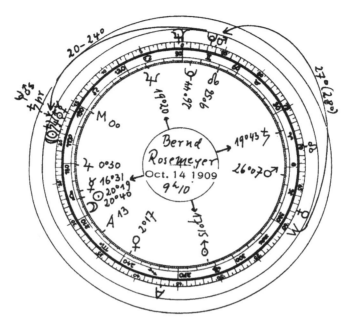

Figure 17. Bernd Rosemeyer.

Uranus-Saturn-Moon. The square of Mars to Pluto with the Ascendant in its axis brings with it dangers, injuries, and accidents. One has to consider whether if, according to tendencies shown in this birth chart, there is an impetus or impulse therein to perform some dangerous feat, thus endangering himself. In carrying out an overall survey, one can see that the moments of danger are indicated around ages twenty-one to twenty-four. When Mars and Pluto reached the constellation of Mercury and the Sun, he was between ages twenty-three and twenty-seven. When Mercury and the Sun crossed the Ascendant-Mars-Pluto, he was ages twenty-six to twenty-seven, it activated the square of Mars-Pluto. It is, however, important to know for this last constellation whether the birth time is accurate. If he was born eight minutes earlier, so that by a solar arc of 28°, the Midheaven = Mars/Pluto = Ascendant, we could state that it would manifest as follows: foolhardy, liable to place himself in danger (Ascendant = Mars/Pluto), and powerless when confronted by exceptional forces and dangers from a force beyond his control (Midheaven = Mars/Pluto = death).

Ruth Litzig

Ruth Litzig was born June 10, 1914, at 12:30 am in Herne, Germany (Figure 18). A swimmer, she first became the town champion in the 110m. breaststroke, then the double champion, and soon after that she was victorious in the 1000m swim in the Rhine-Herne Canal. On August 26, 1932, she set a record by swimming for seventy-three hours and forty-seven minutes, after which she was placed in a car and taken to a hospital where she recovered in a very short time; but she clearly paid for her success. On August 17, 1933, at 11:28 am, she started a new attempt in the Baldeneysee near Essen. The organizers of this attempt were trying everything to keep her awake in the water, but finally, at her request, they allowed her to come out. The doctors then diagnosed hypothermia and severe functional disturbances. Her death followed on August 23, 1933.

Looking at her cosmogram, one can see that this is by no means a convincing example. (The author advocates that one should not pick examples in which the patterns are obvious or can be seen at a glance but rather those by which this method of interpretation can prove itself). The experienced astrologer will see in this cosmogram a drive toward success signified by the opposition of Mars and Jupiter as well as Mars trine Midheaven. Pluto was in the middle of Mars/Uranus (a sudden increase in strength), and Neptune was in the middle of Mars/Pluto and Saturn/Ascendant (a catastrophe to do with water, exclusion from the environment, and malfunction of the skin and sense organs).

Now we must discover whether Ruth at age nineteen was in danger. Using our method, we must not start with the constellation alone, especially as in this case single planetary positions are

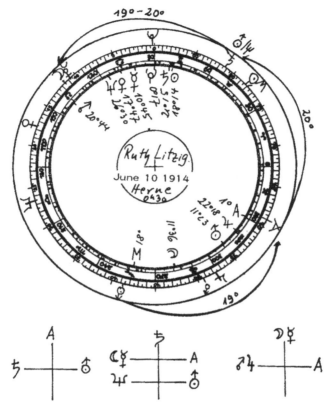

Figure 18. Ruth Litzig.

tolerably well distributed, except for Saturn-Mercury = 19°30',
Ascendant square Saturn = 20°15', Saturn opposition Moon =
20°31', Uranus-Ascendant = 19°37'. If we add a few midpoints,
we thus get Ascendant advanced = Saturn = Uranus/Neptune:
dejection, the need to hold on, pessimism, sadness; Saturn advanced = Moon-Mercury = Mars/Ascendant, an effort to force
success, defeat; and Uranus advanced = Ascendant = Saturn/
Uranus, being in a difficult situation and death. The desire to set
records made her its victim.

Rapid and Reliable Analysis   *51*

Human Failure

*I*t is important to understand the high points in a life, the times of success and recognition, the realization of plans, and the fulfilment of dreams; but it is more essential to recognize in advance the dangers brought by human failure in order to be able to prepare for these. Even if one does not know the exact birth time, such danger points can be recognized if one has a few sign posts from the life of the native.

Oscar Henschel

Oscar Henschel was an industrialist, a descendant of a family whose bell foundry was founded in 1785 in Kassel. The company expanded and became the largest steam locomotive factory in Europe. The first Henschel locomotive was built in 1848. In approximately 1900, the works were completely modernized, and the company later also manufactured trucks, airplanes, and tanks. It can be expected that the owners of such a firm take a great deal of trouble in educating their successors.

Oscar Henschel was born September 1, 1899, in Kassel, Germany (see Figure 19 on page 54). One can immediately see in his cosmogram a Saturn-Pluto opposition. Although this aspect is in the charts of many people born in 1899, in his chart Saturn/Pluto is at the midpoint of Sun/Jupiter; this places a particular burden upon the individual. If one further examines the posi-

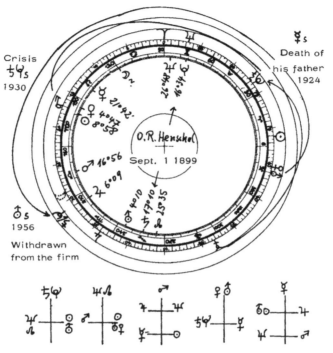

Figure 19. Oscar Henschel.

tions of the planets, one will come to the conclusion that the planetary picture is not a particularly pleasant one. There is likely to be a lack of energy, weakness, an over-estimation of one's own strength, and unsuccessful aims in one's life.

Now let us see how these constellations can be confirmed by his life. On the death of his father, advancing Mercury (with Mars/Neptune advancing = plans without realization) was over Saturn and Pluto. Mars advancing stood in opposition to natal Neptune (= Sun/Mars = energy weakness); Jupiter advancing stood in opposition to Mars (= Jupiter/Neptune = plans without prospect).

In 1929-30, only five years after he took over the management, the firm was threatened with collapse. Saturn advanced and Plu-

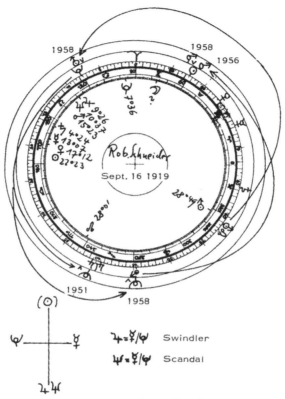

Figure 20. Robert Schneider.

to advanced had reached natal Mars; here again we see the negativity of Mars = Saturn/Pluto. In November 1956 Oscar Robert Henschel was forced to withdraw from the firm. Uranus advancing stood opposite Saturn/Pluto in the natal chart. Thus what is shown in the birth chart is confirmed by the course of his life.

Robert Schneider

Robert Schneider was born September 16, 1919 in Vienna, time available (Figure 20). He became the chief psychologist of the Bundeswehr (militia), and in this position he instructed 700 officers how to carry out tests, the results of which were used in the engagement of officers in the militia; in doing this he deceived his colleagues, the government and the state.

In examining this cosmogram it is obvious that the conjunction of Jupiter with Neptune gains an importance by its position at the midpoint of Mercury/Pluto; according to The Combination of Stellar Influences, this indicates, among other things, a swindler. This constellation would have been instantly recognized if his employers had carried out the practice of examining the cosmogram. It can be seen that the same constellation, Jupiter = Mercury/Pluto, is in the cosmogram of the swindler Karl Heinz Bohm (not to be confused with the actor of the same name).

This constellation played a special role in the life of Robert Schneider. He was arrested for the first time when advancing Pluto reached Jupiter/Neptune and Neptune transited Mercury. When he came to the Bundeswehr in 1956, one could have seen that Mars advancing had moved toward the position of the Sun, thus activating the planetary picture mentioned above. When in 1958 this process was completed, Mars advancing stood exactly in the axis of these planets.

***

When people cannot make anything out of themselves or their destiny, they often commit suicide. Out of our many cases the following are taken.

Suicide by Poison

This woman, born March 20, 1923, at 9:00 pm in Muhlacker, Germany, poisoned herself during the morning of June 20, 1949, by drinking muriatic acid. Her death came soon after noon. Her parents and relatives were unable to understand this act (Figure 21).

On the 90°-chart the constellation Mars-Venus-Jupiter stands out. Neptune is fairly close to the midpoint of Mars/Jupiter. In

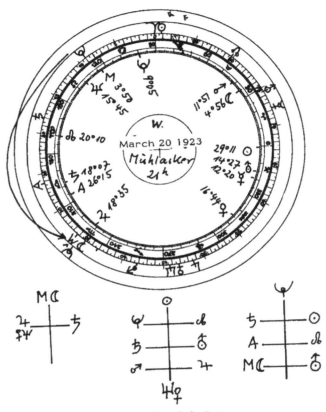

Figure 21. Suicide by Poison.

*The Combination of Stellar Influence*s the following interpretation is given: inferiority, falsehood, unfaithfulness, aims without a chance of their realization. This cosmic picture is of importance because of the opposition to the Sun and its equidistance from Pluto-Node-Mercury-Saturn-Uranus. From all of these we select for interpretation Sun = Neptune = Saturn/Uranus, which is given as: to expose the body to severe tests of strength, psychological tensions, suffering of the soul, unable to stand, giving up of resistance, weakening of strength, separation, and death.

Rapid and Reliable Analysis   57

Further constellations should also be noted: Saturn-Pluto-Sun indicates an obstruction in development through illness, a weakening. Also see Pluto = Sun/Saturn = Node/Ascendant = Uranus/Midheaven = Moon/Mercury: perception of tragedy, associations which have a strange destiny, collapse through overwork, these are only a few points. The combination of Moon/Midheaven is also of note. One can see that these are in the axis between Saturn and the Jupiter-Venus constellation; when interpreted this gives easily aggravated, likes to be alone, inhibitions, dissatisfied, emotional depressions, suffering of the soul and easily discouraged, soul illness. This interpretation can be found in *The Combination of Stellar Influences*. These tendencies will become active if a single planet or a whole constellation transits any one of these. This was the case when Saturn after twenty-seven years transited Neptune, reached Mercury, and later transited Uranus.

The same probabilities result with the Sun passing over Saturn after 19° of progression and after 34° over the Midheaven and after that the Moon; if Pluto is advanced 25° it reaches the Midheaven and the Moon. In accordance with our method, there would seem to be a severe crisis indicated between the twenty-fifth and twenty-seventh year of life. This should not have led to suicide, had it been recognized and all the necessary precautions taken. Using a solar arc of 25°47', Pluto advanced (= Sun/Saturn advancing = Uranus/Midheaven) was in 4 Leo 52 and went over the square to the Moon in 4°56' (= Midheaven = Saturn/Neptune, Venus, Jupiter). This is to within a four-minute accuracy. The tendency to depression is confirmed through the time of suicide, and this also confirms the value of the rapid analysis and proves it to be a reliable method.

As has been shown in *Anatomrsche Entsprechungen der Tierkreisgrade* (The Relationship of the Zodiac Degrees to Anatomy), if a cosmological enquiry were made in association with physicians and the psychologists, it might be possible to prevent such tragedies and to take the necessary precautions.

Reinhold Ebertin

Short Examples

A deep insight into the system of rapid and reliable analysis can only be gained by the study of many birth charts, and the examples so far presented only show us how we can get the fastest possible result. To get a greater insight, we give here some examples that are in a condensed but understandable form. We place an emphasis on the basic construction of the birth chart, and then its activation indicating an event.

Only through careful comparison and accurate examination of cases that are similar can one gain the certainty that is required by the scientist. The author has not selected examples for a specific purpose but has taken interesting cases and placed them in such an order so that a particular point is emphasized.

The first few examples are chosen to demonstrate success and in each case the Sun advanced was in aspect to natal Jupiter, or the reverse. An aspect between the Sun and Jupiter has always been considered favorable; other interpretations can be given as recognition, success, a rise in the world.

The character of such an activation will first of all be dependent upon the cosmic condition of the Sun and Jupiter but also it will depend upon the environment in which the person was born.

Most of Hildegard Knef's (Figure 22) abilities are the result of the relationship between the Sun and Jupiter. An artist, it is unimportant that at times she was less successful because we are here only studying the Sun and Jupiter constellations as a single item, and thus limiting the period studied. A success is a success, whether it is material or mental.

It does not matter how success was achieved; all that is necessary to understand, is the relationship of Sun/Jupiter, as in the case of Ludwig Hoelscher (Figure 23) where it led to his success, when he was nominated as a professor. In the case of the author Erich Maria Remarque (Figure 24), he was very successful. Captain Hermann Kohl, a pilot (Figure 25) demonstrated this constellation by a transoceanic flight. The Duchess of Windsor (Figure 26), who had been divorced, married the son of a king and became a duchess. In some of these examples one can see that Venus/Uranus, musical rhythm, is evident. In the case of Remarque, Venus related to Pluto produced an influence upon the masses; in the case of Kohl the Sun and Uranus led him toward technical performance, and the Duchess of Windsor had luck in love through Venus/Jupiter.

The Jupiter/Pluto configurations produce plutonic luck, as can be seen in the case of the Begum Aga Khan (Figure 27). This case is similar to that of the Duchess of Windsor where Jupiter and Venus were involved. Wernher Von Braun (Figure 28), was a rocket specialist who lived to see plutonic luck in the scientific field. He collaborated on the German V1 rocket and later emigrated to the United States, where he rose socially and was recognized as one of the great scientists. One should observe here the constellation of Mars-Pluto-Sun, which frequently occurs in the cosmograms of atomic scientists and rocket specialists.

Relationships between Pluto and the Midheaven can mean unusual changes or appointments. However, the single example shown here indicates a fundamental difference. In the case of the Begum Aga Khan (Figure 29), her elevation to the status of an Indian princess followed marriage, whereas Juliana, queen of Holland (Figure 30) came to the throne under this constellation.

Reinhold Ebertin

In the case of General De Gaulle (Figures 31, 32, and 33), he was not only promoted to general but he felt it was his mission to organize the resistance in France and to take over the leadership of his people. It will be seen from the figures how De Gaulle was affected by the combination of Jupiter/Pluto in both these events. The axis of Jupiter/Pluto transits Mercury, and the Midheaven advances to enters the radical axis. Richard Wagner (Figure 34), was called to Munich by King Ludwig under the influence of Pluto advancing = Midheaven and through this fulfilled many different plans. In the spiritual and religious area we find the cases of Therese Neumann (Figure 35) and Pater Pio (Figure 36), both of whom experienced the stigmata, while in the case of St. Theresa of Lisieux (Figure 37) she felt it necessary to enter a convent.

In these cases it should not be overlooked that Saturn was involved. According to *The Combination of Stellar Influences*, Saturn-Pluto-Midheaven signifies self sacrifice and asceticism. The author has to admit that he could not get over his amazement when examining these cases, for despite forty years in the practice of this science, he could feel nothing but wonder when he recognized the wonderful relationship that can be seen between the cosmic constellations and the earthly experience.

The example of Wallenstein (Figure 38) is given because the cosmic picture at the time of his murder is very clear; it is sufficient even to convert a skeptic. The last cases presented here show how tendencies toward sickness can arise at certain times when a constellation is activated. This does not mean that the illness has to be experienced, particularly if prevention/treatment occurs early enough after the recognition of those tendencies in the cosmogram; then one has an opportunity to avoid it. These cases of illness and disease are taken from Anatomical Correspondence in the Zodiac and serve only to illustrate the correlation between a tendency and an activation. It will be clearly seen how a single constellation, or one in relationship to another, can show the stimulation of an event.

Rapid and Reliable Analysis   61

When there is a relationship between single zodiacal signs that indicates a confirmation, we must check this correlation against the birth chart and not be misled into wrong decisions. It has not been possible in this treatise to examine each cosmogram from all its many aspects and to examine all the minute detail because it became obvious to the author that there was a greater importance in teaching the eye to recognize the essentials in a birth chart and to grasp the possibility that an activation could occur. Because each figure in the birth chart is a totality in itself, one must always be careful to see the whole with all it single parts. In this way one will learn and understand that there is no other science in which the nature of man and his past, present, and future—in fact the foundation of his entire development—can be simultaneously seen. In order to come to such a total presentation based upon cosmic structures, one must not only accumulate knowledge and experience but also exchange this information; this includes an interchange with all other sciences, in which cosmobiology as we understand it will act as a connecting link and not work in isolation.

Those who may have believed that the relationship of man with the infinite cosmos does not exist must know that this cosmic tie has been reconfirmed through scientific investigation. Concerning this, let us remember the closing sentence of Hans Stossel's article: "It is essential today to come to a deeper spiritual, cosmic understanding, and that this alone is the necessity of our age, and the need of this century should be revelation. This should be a time when man stands with a greater knowledge (not only a belief) of how to be at one with the universe."

The author of Atom and Psyche, Von Eickstedt, expresses this with a great deal of certainty: "The psyche goes back upon the atom; follows its power and from it then moves towards its opposite. This means action of the eternal in the temporal. The soul originates in the universe and this taken fundamentally is self evident."

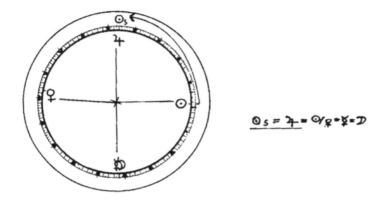

Figure 22. Hildegard Knef.

Hildegard Knef, Actress

Natal: Jupiter = Node = Sun/Venus = Moon = Mercury (successful artist).

Activation: Sun advanced (= Moon/Jupiter advanced = Mercury/Jupiter advanced) = natal Jupiter.

Events: Great success, recognition as best actress of 194 7.

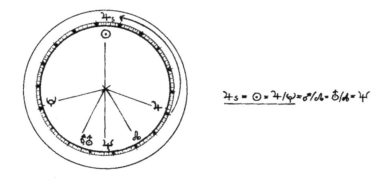

$$2\!\!\!/_s = \odot = 2\!\!\!/\psi = \sigma^*/\Omega = \hat{\odot}/\Omega = \text{H}$$

Figure 23. Ludwig Hoelscher.

Ludwig Hoelscher, Cellist

Natal: Jupiter = Venus/Uranus = Venus/Mars (love of art, sense of rhythm, artistic temperament).

Activation: Jupiter advanced = natal Sun (= Jupiter/Pluto= Mars/Node).

Events: Great success, promoted to professor at age twenty-nine.

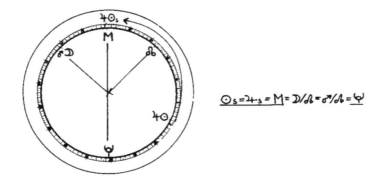

$$\underline{\odot}_s = \underline{4}_s = M = \mathcal{D}/\Omega = \sigma/\Omega = \underline{\Psi}$$

Figure 24. Erich Maria Remarque.

Erich Maria Remarque, Author

Natal: Jupiter = Sun = Node/Pluto = Midheaven/Uranus = Venus (riches, success in art).

Activation: Jupiter advanced = Sun advanced = natal Midheaven (= Pluto = Mars/Node).

Events: Worldwide success of *All Quiet on the Western Front*.

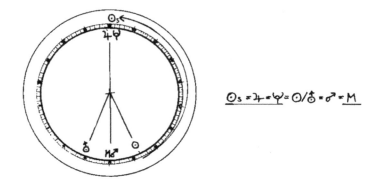

$$\underline{\odot}_s = 2\!\!\!+ = \psi = \odot/\hat{\delta} = \sigma^7 = \underline{M}$$

Figure 25. Hermann Kohl.

Hermann Kohl, Pilot

Natal: Jupiter = Pluto = Mars = Midheaven = Sun/Uranus (successful inventor, technician, reaching aims, ability to achieve).

Activation: Sun advanced = Jupiter = Pluto = Mars = Midheaven = Sun/Uranus.

Events: Great success, created a sensation as the first transoceanic pilot from Germany.

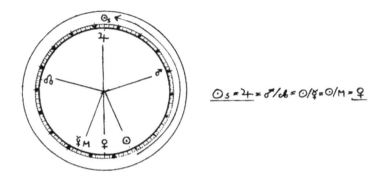

$$\underline{\odot_s} \, * \, 2\!\!\!+ = \, \delta/cb = \odot/\xi = \odot/M * \, \underline{\varphi}$$

Figure 26. Wallis, Duchess of Windsor.

Wallis, Duchess of Windsor

Natal: Jupiter = Venus = Mars/Node (happy love match), Sun = Moon/Midheaven = Moon/Mercury = Ascendant/Midheaven = Jupiter/Uranus (strong soul link, relationship with the public, far sighted, good luck).

Activation: Sun advanced = Jupiter = natal Venus.

Events: Twice divorced; but despite this, she married the Duke of Windsor).

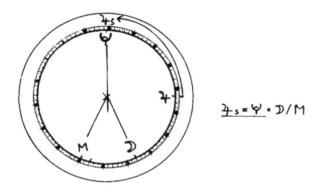

Figure 27. Begum Aga Khan.

Begum Aga Khan, Indian Princess

Natal: Jupiter = Venus = Sun Pluto/M. C. (Unusual success, the power to follow through).

Activation: Jupiter advanced = natal Pluto (= Moon/Midheaven).

Events: Great success as a model and beauty queen in France. This was the start of an unusual rise in social standing).

Reinhold Ebertin

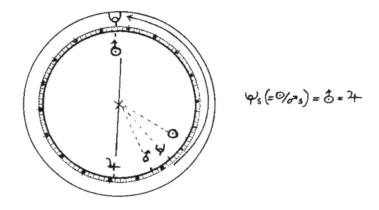

Figure 28. Wernher Von Braun.

Wernher Von Braun, Rocket Specialist

Natal: Pluto = Sun/Mars (created a formula for rocket and atomic scientists) = Ascendant = Uranus/Midheaven (fanatical ambition), Jupiter= Uranus (inventor) =Sun/Moon.

Activation: Pluto advanced = Jupiter.

Events: First launch of the V1 rocket, emigrated to the United States, where he became a prominent space scientist.

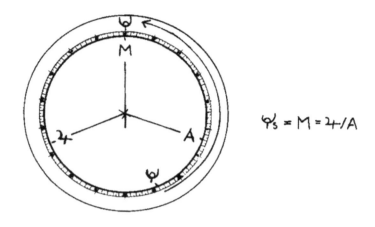

$$\m%s = M = 2\!\!+\!/A$$

Figure 29. Begum Aga Khan.

Begun Aga Khan, Indian Princess

Natal: Midheaven = Jupiter/Ascendant = Sun/Ascendant = Venus/Ascendant (harmonious personality, move to comfortable surroundings, unusual rise in social status).

Activation: Pluto advanced = natal Midheaven.

Events: Marriage to the Aga Khan, unusual rise in social status.

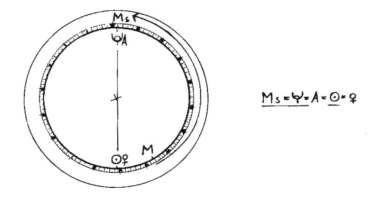

Figure 30. Juliana, Queen of Holland.

Juliana, Queen of Holland

Natal: Pluto = Sun = Ascendant = Venus (power and drive, ability to follow through, popularity, ability to control the environment), Midheaven = Mercury/Mars = Moon/Uranus (readiness to act, decisiveness).

Activation: Midheaven advanced = natal Pluto.

Events: Accession to the throne (calling).

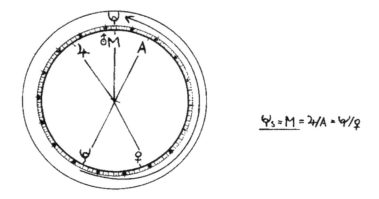

Figure 31. Charles De Gaulle.

Charles De Gaulle, President of France

Natal: Midheaven = Uranus = Jupiter/Ascendant (achieves his aims, success), Pluto = Moon/ Jupiter = Moon/ Mars = Ascendant = Sun/Node = Sun/Saturn (large undertakings, fanaticism, the taking over of leadership, influencing the masses).

Activation: Pluto advanced = Midheaven.

Events: Youngest general in French army, organized the resistance in France 1940-1942.

Reinhold Ebertin

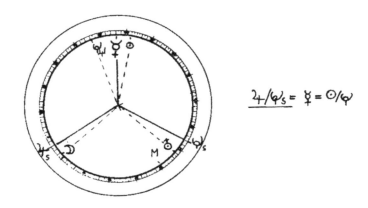

$$\underline{2\!+\!/\varphi_s} = \yen = \odot/\varphi$$

Figure 32. Charles De Gaulle.

Charles De Gaulle, President of France

Natal: Mercury = Sun/Pluto = Sun/Neptune = Moon/Uranus = Moon/Midheaven. (Drive toward spiritual leadership, leadership, prudence, organizational ability, purposefulness, power of suggestion).

Activation: Natal Mercury = Jupiter/Pluto advanced.

Events: Took power in France in 1945.

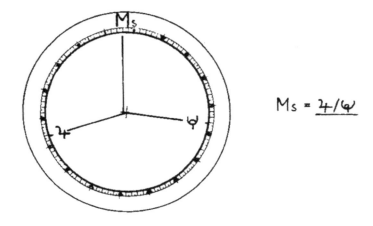

$$Ms = \frac{2\!\!\!\!/ / \mathcal{Q}}{}$$

Figure 33. Charles De Gaulle.

Charles De Gaulle, President of France

Natal: Midheaven (leadership). Jupiter/Pluto (drive for power in attaining a leadership position—not in the birth chart, but activated in 1945 and 1948).

Activation: Midheaven advanced = natal Jupiter/Pluto.

Reinhold Ebertin

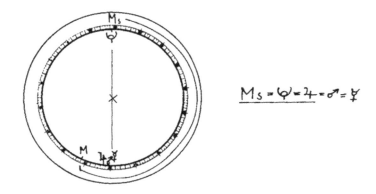

Figure 34. Richard Wagner.

Richard Wagner, Composer

Natal: Pluto = Mercury = Mars = Jupiter (success, power of suggestion; the ability of developing one's strength).

Activation: Midheaven advanced = Pluto

Events: Called to Munich by King Ludwig.

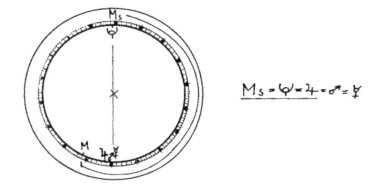

Figure 35. Therese Neumann.

Therese Neumann, Stigmata

Natal: Pluto = Sun/Mercury = Uranus/Neptune = Mars/Saturn (suggestion working through physical suffering, transcendental manifestations). Natal Midheaven = Sun/ Jupiter = Mercury/Saturn = Mercury /Pluto (religious, serious, suggestive, effective).

Activation: Pluto advanced = natal Midheaven = Saturn advanced.

Events: Feeling for a vocation, commencement of the stigmata.

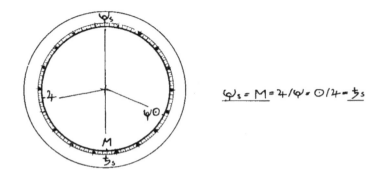

Figure 36. Pater Pius.

Pater Pius, Stigmata

Natal: Sun/Mercury = Saturn (serious life, suggestion), Midheaven = Sun/Jupiter= Mars/Ascendant = Neptune/Ascendant (religious, a fighter, a sensitive person).

Activation: Pluto advanced = natal Midheaven = Saturn advanced.

Events: The feeling of a vocation, the start of the stigmata.

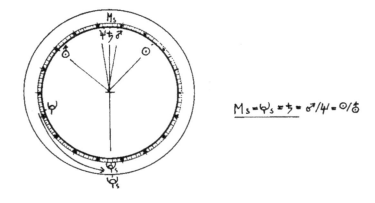

$$M_s = \Psi_s = \hbar = \sigma^7/4 = \odot/\delta$$

Figure 37. St. Therese of Lisieux.

St. Therese of Lisieux

Natal: Saturn = Mars/Neptune = Sun/Uranus (lack of energy for living, sudden separation). Midheaven = Pluto = Moon/Uranus = Mercury/ Mars = Mercury/Saturn = Mercury = Neptune (inner change, vocation, willfulness, concentrated thinking, unusual problems, active unconscious).

Activation: Midheaven advanced = Pluto advanced = natal Saturn.

Events: Vocation, entered a convent.

Reinhold Ebertin

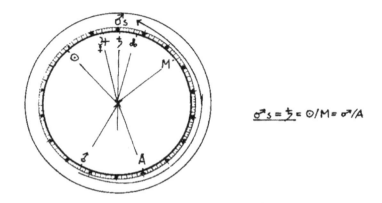

Figure 38. Albrecht Von Wallenstein.

Albrecht Von Wallenstein, Army Commander

Natal: Mars = Jupiter/Midheaven = Mercury/Midheaven = Saturn/Midheaven (creative power, reflection, the ability to submit to destiny), Saturn = Mercury /Node = Sun/Midheaven = Mars/Ascendant (difficult decisions, defeat).

Activation: Mars advanced = Saturn.

Event: Murdered.

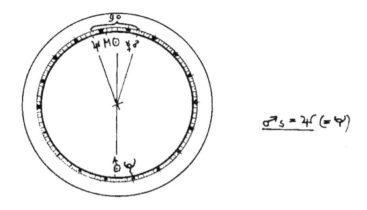

Figure 39. Infantile Paralysis.

Infantile Paralysis

Natal: Uranus = 17 Aries (spinal cord). Sun = Midheaven = Mars/Neptune = Uranus (undermining of health, sudden bouts of weakness, crisis).

Activation: Mars advanced = Neptune (= Pluto).

Events: Onset of infantile paralysis; treatment successful, but left paralysis in the hands.

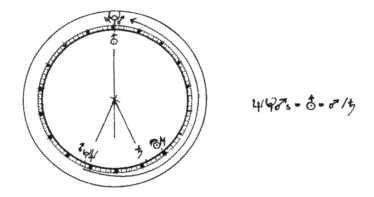

Figure 40. Contraction of the Liver.

Contraction of the Liver

Natal: Sun = Venus (24 Virgo = liver) = Moon= Saturn/Midheaven. (Difficulties with others, depression, sickness through psychological suffering). Uranus = Mars/Saturn = Saturn/Neptune = Saturn/Pluto (sudden illness, death).

Activation: Pluto advanced (Mars/Neptune advanced) = Uranus (= Mars/Saturn).

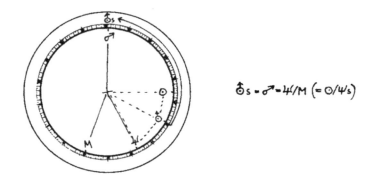

$\hat{\odot}s - \sigma - 4/M \ (= \odot/4s)$

Figure 41. Festering Wound.

Festering Wound

Natal: Uranus (5 Aquarius = calf of leg) = Sun/Neptune = Mars/ Pluto (infection, illness, accident, injury). Mars = Neptune/ Midheaven (insecurity).

Activation: Uranus advanced = natal Mars.

Events: Ulcers on lower leg, wound, arm injury (Saturn in Gem- ini advanced = Midheaven).

Reinhold Ebertin

9 780866 900935